T0143895

BEFORE USING...

 Before using this book, please read the guidelines inside the back cover. For a free copy of the detailed guidelines go to www.hunterhouse.com or call the ordering number below.

 To prevent bleed-through, it is recommended that water-based, rather than spirit-based, markers or pens be used in this Workbook.

MY OWN THOUGHTS ON STOPPING THE HURT

A Hunter House Growth and Recovery Workbook
by Wendy Deaton, M.A., M.F.C.C.
Series consultant: Kendall Johnson, Ph.D.

ISBN-10: 1-63026-805-4   ISBN-13: 978-1-63026-805-3

COPYRIGHT INFORMATION
Text and illustrations © Wendy Deaton 1993
Design and layout © Hunter House 1993
Cover illustration by Cecilia Bowman

First U.S. edition published in 1993 by Hunter House

All rights reserved. No part of this Workbook or Therapist Guide may be reproduced or transmitted in any form or by any means, electronic or mechanical, including photocopying or recording, nor may it be introduced into any information storage and retrieval system without the written permission of the copyright owner and the publisher of this book.

The publisher grants a limited reproduction license to individuals and institutions who have purchased a workbook to duplicate pages as needed for use at one single location. Any further duplication and distribution is a violation of copyright and is prohibited. For further information contact Hunter House Inc.

10 9 8 7   First Edition   12 13 14 15

ORDERING INFORMATION

Additional copies of this and other Growth and Recovery Workbooks may be obtained from Hunter House. Bulk discounts are available for professional offices and recognized organizations.

All single workbooks: $11.95

THE GROWTH AND RECOVERY WORKBOOKS (GROW) SERIES

A creative, child-friendly program designed for use with elementary-school children, filled with original exercises to foster healing, self-understanding, and optimal growth.

Workbooks for children ages 9–12 include:

No More Hurt—provides a safe place for children who have been physically or sexually abused to explore and share their feelings

Living with My Family—helps children traumatized by domestic violence and family fights to identify and express their fears

Someone I Love Died—for children who have lost a loved one and who are dealing with grief, loss, and helplessness

A Separation in My Family—for children whose parents are separating or have already separated or divorced

Drinking and Drugs in My Family—for children who have family members who engage in regular alcohol and substance abuse

I Am a Survivor—for children who have survived an accident or fire, or a natural disaster such as a flood, hurricane, or earthquake

I Saw It Happen—for children who have witnessed a traumatic event such as a shooting at school, a frightening accident, or other violence

Workbooks for children ages 6–10 include:

My Own Thoughts and Feelings (for Girls); My Own Thoughts and Feelings (for Boys)—for exploring suspected trauma and early symptoms of depression, low self-esteem, family conflict, maladjustment, and nonspecific dysfunction

My Own Thoughts on Stopping the Hurt—for exploring suspected trauma and communicating with young children who may have suffered physical or sexual abuse

We welcome suggestions for new and needed workbooks

DISCLAIMER

This book is intended as a treatment tool for use in a therapeutic setting. It is not intended to be utilized for diagnostic or investigative purposes. It is not designed for and should not be recommended or suggested for use in any unsupervised or self-help or self-therapy setting, group, or situation whatsoever. Any professionals who use this book are exercising their own professional judgment and take full responsibility for doing so.

You are SPECIAL.

Write your name here.

©1993 Wendy Deaton and Hunter House Inc.

Make a list of special things about yourself.

_____

_____

_____

_____

_____

_____

_____

_____

_____

_____

©1993 Wendy Deaton and Hunter House Inc.

©1993 Wendy Deaton and Hunter House Inc.

Draw a picture of
how you feel
today.

Complete the following lines:

Something that scares me is

_____

_____

Something that makes me happy is

_____

_____

I feel mad when

_____

_____

I feel sad when

_____

_____

I feel bad when

_____

_____

I feel good when

_____

_____

©1993 Wendy Deaton and Hunter House Inc.

What is the most
important thing
you want people
to know about you?

What is the most
important thing
you don't want
people to know
about you?

©1993 Wendy Deaton and Hunter House Inc.

Something scary has happened to you. Someone hurt you.

When something like this happens it causes a problem.

Problems make you feel angry, scared, or helpless. Some problems will change your life forever.

This book is about problems kids have about being hurt. It will help you understand what happened and feel stronger, safer, and happier in the future.

On the next page are some FEELINGS people have about problems. ➜

©1993 Wendy Deaton and Hunter House Inc.

SADNESS: Feelings that hurt and make you want to cry.

LONELINESS: Feeling no one understands you. Not wanting to talk to anybody or be with anybody, or not having anybody to talk to.

FEAR: Being scared about many things.

GUILT: Feeling as if you did something bad, or like you should be punished for what happened.

DENYING: Pretending, believing, or wishing it didn't happen.

CONFUSION: Not understanding what happened. Not understanding your feelings, or having a lot of different feelings at one time.

ANGER: Wanting to kick, bite, hit, push. Blaming other people. Wishing bad things about other people, or wanting to hurt someone else.

These are all normal feelings. Everyone who has problems feels these feelings sometimes.

©1993 Wendy Deaton and Hunter House Inc.

Write or draw about what happened to you. Tell what you saw, what you heard, anything you smelled, anything that was different or strange. Tell about your thoughts.

©1993 Wendy Deaton and Hunter House Inc.

©1993 Wendy Deaton and Hunter House Inc.

Write about all
the feelings you
had when you
first got hurt.

©1993 Wendy Deaton and Hunter House Inc.

©1993 Wendy Deaton and Hunter House Inc.

What are some
feelings you
have <u>now</u> about
this problem?

Why do you think
this happened to
you? Write all
the reasons you
can think of.

©1993 Wendy Deaton and Hunter House Inc.

Here are some important things
you should know:

▲ What happened is
   NOT YOUR FAULT.

▲ You did not want this
   problem to happen
   —it just happened.

▲ You did not cause
   this problem.

▲ Sometimes bad
   things happen to
   good people.

©1993 Wendy Deaton and Hunter House Inc.

Who have you told about this
problem?

_____

_____

_____

How did they act when you told
them?

_____

_____

_____

What is the most helpful thing
someone said or did to help you?

_____

_____

_____

©1993 Wendy Deaton and Hunter House Inc.

Some people may act angry or scared when you try to talk about what happened to you. Other people may pretend that nothing important happened to you.

If someone makes you feel unhappy, guilty, or embarrassed, don't talk to them anymore about what happened. Find someone to talk to who makes you feel better.

Make a list of all the helpers in your life that you can talk to about this problem.

©1993 Wendy Deaton and Hunter House Inc.

Problems can change
people. Write or draw
a picture of how
you were before
this problem.

©1993 Wendy Deaton and Hunter House Inc.

Write or draw a picture of how this problem changed you. Show the changes you like and the changes you don't like.

©1993 Wendy Deaton and Hunter House Inc.

When you have been hurt
it is natural to want to cry.
Your sadness may seem so big,
and worried feelings so great,
that you think things will
never get better.

You may even wish you
had never been born,
or that you could die now
so the sadness would stop.
Even though you feel this
way now, try to remember—

things
will get
BETTER
in time

©1993 Wendy Deaton and Hunter House Inc.

©1993 Wendy Deaton and Hunter House Inc.

Write about any sad
feelings you have
or thoughts you
have about not
wanting to live
with your sadness.

Nightmares are scary,
mixed-up dreams that
worry you.

Write or draw a
picture of a bad
dream or nightmare
you have had.

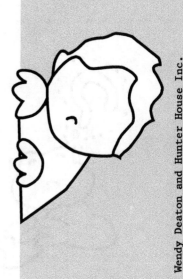

©1993 Wendy Deaton and Hunter House Inc.

If you have been hurt, you may think about it a lot. You may have trouble thinking about other things. Even if you like school, you may not be able to think about learning.

Write about any trouble you are having with your thinking.

©1993 Wendy Deaton and Hunter House Inc.

You may feel like getting even with the person who hurt you.

It is okay to feel angry, as long as you don't break something, hurt yourself, or hurt someone else.

Angry feelings are normal when you are hurt. If someone has hurt you, you may feel angry a lot.

Draw an angry picture.

©1993 Wendy Deaton and Hunter House Inc.

If you have feelings toward someone and you haven't told them, you can write your feelings now. You can write to the person who hurt you, or to someone who helped you.

©1993 Wendy Deaton and Hunter House Inc.

Write or draw about how
you wish things had
turned out with this
problem, instead of
what really
did happen.

©1993 Wendy Deaton and Hunter House Inc.

Something good can happen even with a
bad problem.
Maybe you feel braver, stronger,
smarter now.
Maybe you made some new friends, or
found out more people care about you
than you thought.

Write about anything GOOD
that happened.

©1993 Wendy Deaton and Hunter House Inc.

Do you agree ✓ or disagree ✗

☐ Life is always happy.

☐ Life means always being safe.

☐ Life is sometimes scary.

☐ Life sometimes hurts.

☐ Everyone makes mistakes.

☐ Children don't deserve
to be hurt.

☐ Sometimes bad things happen to
good people.

☐ Life is good, even though bad
things happen.

☐ Life is worth living.

©1993 Wendy Deaton and Hunter House Inc.

If you were in a race what kind would it be?

- [ ] running
- [ ] car
- [ ] bike
- [ ] horses
- [ ] motorcycle
- [ ] skateboard
- [ ] skis

What others?

_____

_____

_____

What would you need to win?

- [ ] patience
- [ ] practice
- [ ] strength
- [ ] bravery
- [ ] speed
- [ ] luck
- [ ] brains

These things can help you now to feel safer and stronger and happier in your life.

©1993 Wendy Deaton and Hunter House Inc.

Write or draw about a favorite memory
you have from before you were hurt.
This memory will help
remind you that life
in the past was good.

©1993 Wendy Deaton and Hunter House Inc.

©1993 Wendy Deaton and Hunter House Inc.

Write or draw about a happy or good memory you have from after you got hurt. This will remind you the future can still be good.

You don't have to be unhappy forever.
You cannot fix or change what
happened, but as time passes,
you will see you can feel better.

Make a list of all the things that
would make you happier now.

_____

_____

_____

_____

_____

_____

_____

_____

©1993 Wendy Deaton and Hunter House Inc.

Make a list of things you can do for yourself to make you happier now.

©1993 Wendy Deaton and Hunter House Inc.

Hope means
believing things
can get better.
Write a story
about HOPE.

©1993 Wendy Deaton and Hunter House Inc.

PLEASE READ THIS...

This is a brief guide to the design and use of the Growth and Recovery (GROW) workbooks from Hunter House. It is excerpted from detailed guidelines that can be downloaded from www .hunterhouse.com or are available free through the mail by calling the ordering number at the bottom of the page. Please consult the detailed guidelines before using this workbook for the first time.

GROW workbooks provide a way to open up communication with children who are not able to or who are reluctant to talk about a traumatic experience. They are not self-help books and are not designed for guardians or parents to use on their own with children. They address sensitive issues, and a child's recovery and healing require the safety, structured approach, and insight provided by a trained professional.

Each therapist will bring her own originality, creativity, and experience to the interaction and may adapt the tasks and activities in the workbooks, using other materials and activities. With less verbally oriented children, the use of art therapy or music or video may be recommended, or certain exercises may be conducted in groups.

Each pair of facing pages in the workbook provides the focus for a therapeutic "movement" that may take up one session. However, more than one movement can be made in a single session or several sessions may be devoted to a single movement. Children should be allowed to move through the process at their own pace. If a child finds a task too "hot" to approach, the therapist can return to it later. When something is fruitful it can be pursued with extended tasks.

While a therapist is free to select the order of activities for each child, the exercises are laid out in a progression based on the principles of critical incident stress management:

- initial exercises focus on building the therapeutic alliance
- the child is then led to relate an overview of the experience
- this is deepened by a "sensory-unpacking" designed to access and recover traumatic memories
- family experiences and changed living conditions, if any, are explored
- emotions are encouraged, explored, and validated.
- delayed reactions are dealt with, and resources are explored.
- the experience is integrated into the child's life through a series of strength-building exercises.

Specific pages in the GROW workbooks are cross-referenced to Dr. Kendall Johnson's book *Trauma in the Lives of Children* (Hunter House, Alameda, 1998). This provides additional information on the treatment of traumatized children.

The content of the workbooks should be shared with parents or significant adults only when the child feels ready for it and if it is therapeutically wise. Workbooks should not be given to children to take home until the therapeutic process is completed according to the therapist's satisfaction.

Although this series of workbooks was written for school-age children, the tasks are adaptable for use with younger children and adolescents.

©2007 Wendy Deaton, Kendall Johnson, and Hunter House

Detailed guidelines are available for each GROW workbook (see list on front inside cover).

Printed in the USA
CPSIA information can be obtained
at www.ICGtesting.com
JSHW050802160824
68134JS00069B/113

9 781630 268053